KLASSISCHE MEISTERWERKE ZUM KENNENLERNEN ✷ GET TO KNOW CLASSICAL MASTERPIECES

Antonio Vivaldi

(1678–1741)

Die vier Jahreszeiten

Konzerte für Violine, Streicher und Basso continuo
op. 8 Nr. 1–4

Für Klavier leicht bearbeitet von
Hans-Günter Heumann

Deutsche Übertragung der Sonette
von Ingrid Hermann

Zeichnungen von Brigitte Smith

The Four Seasons

Concertos for violin, strings and basso continuo
Op. 8 Nos. 1–4

In a simple arrangement for piano
by Hans-Günter Heumann

English version of the poems
by Julia Rushworth

Drawings by Brigitte Smith

ED 23584
ISMN 979-0-001-21589-3
ISBN 978-3-7957-2595-2

SCHOTT

Mainz · London · Madrid · Paris · New York · Tokyo · Beijing

Liebe Klavierspielerin, lieber Klavierspieler,

in diesem Band wird eines der bekanntesten und schönsten Konzerte des Barock, *Die vier Jahreszeiten* von Antonio Vivaldi (1678–1741), in leichter Bearbeitung für Klavier vorgestellt.

Die vier Jahreszeiten sind die ersten vier von zwölf Konzerten aus dem Opus 8. Alle Konzerte sind dreisätzig mit den typischen Ecksätzen in Ritornellform (ital. ritorno = Wiederkehr; meist mehrfach wiederkehrender Abschnitt, im Solokonzert des 18. Jahrhunderts die Tutti-Abschnitte, im Gegensatz zu den Solo-Episoden) und einem langsamen Mittelsatz. Jedem Konzert ist ein vermutlich von Vivaldi selbst verfasstes 14-zeiliges Sonett vorangestellt, das die jeweilige Jahreszeit charakterisiert und so, wie Vivaldi dazu bemerkt, „... die Musik leichter erklärt".
Aber nun lasst euch von den ausdrucksstarken Naturschilderungen Vivaldis verzaubern.

Euer
Hans-Günter Heumann

Dear Pianists,

In this volume you will find a simple arrangement for piano of one of the best known and loveliest concertos of the Baroque era, *The Four Seasons* by Antonio Vivaldi (1678–1741).

The Four Seasons are the first four of twelve concertos included in Opus 8. All the concertos have three movements, typically having the outer movements in ritornello form (Italian ritorno = return, usually a section recurring several times; in the solo concerto of the 18th century this meant the tutti sections, contrasting with the solo episodes) and a slow middle movement. Each concerto is prefaced with a 14-line sonnet, presumably written by Vivaldi himself, which characterizes the season in question and thus, as Vivaldi himself commented, "... helps to explain the music".
But now allow yourselves to be enchanted by Vivaldi's expressive depictions of nature.

With best wishes,
Hans-Günter Heumann

Inhalt

Contents

Steckbrief
Die vier Jahreszeiten

Komponiert zwischen 1700 und 1725

Gewidmet Graf Wenzeslav von Marzin

Originaltitel auf italienisch Le quattro stagioni
(La primavera, L'estate, L'autunno, L'inverno)

veröffentlicht 1725 in Amsterdam vom Verleger
Michel Charles Le Cene in der Sammlung von
12 Konzerten op. 8 „Il cimento dell' armonia e
dell' invenzione" (Das Wagnis der Harmonie und
der Erfindung)

Orchesterbesetzung Violine I und II, Viola, Basso
continuo (Cembalo, Violoncello und Kontrabass ad
libitum)

History of the work
The Four Seasons

Composed between 1700 and 1725

Dedicated to Count Wenceslav von Marzin

Original title in Italian Le quattro stagioni
(La primavera, L'estate, L'autunno, L' inverno)

Published in Amsterdam in 1725 by Michel
Charles Le Cene in the collection of 12 concertos
Op. 8 "Il cimento dell'armonia e dell' invenzione"
(The testing of harmony and invention)

Orchestration violins I and II, viola, basso continuo (harpsichord, cello and double bass ad libitum)

Steckbrief
Antonio Vivaldi

1678 geboren am 4. März in Venedig;
Musikunterricht durch den Vater, der Geiger
am Markusdom in Venedig war

1692 Beginn der Priesterlaufbahn

1703 wird er zum Priester geweiht und anschlie-
ßend zum Hauskomponist am Ospedale della Pietà
ernannt; erste Komposition, durch die er bald euro-
päischen Ruf erlangt

1717 Kammerkapellmeister in Mantua

ab 1729 viele Konzertreisen durch Europa

1740 lässt sich in Wien nieder

1741 stirbt am 28. Juli in Wien

Biography
Antonio Vivaldi

1678 born in Venice on 4 March; he was given
music lessons by his father, who was a violinist at
St Mark's Basilica in Venice

1692 he began training for a career as a priest

1703 he was ordained as a priest and subsequently
appointed composer in residence at the Ospedale
della Pietà; his first compositions were published,
rapidly establishing his reputation throughout
Europe

1717 Director of chamber music in Mantua

from 1729 numerous concert tours across Europe

1740 he settled in Vienna

1741 he died in Vienna on 28 July

La primavera
Der Frühling ‖ Spring
op. 8/1

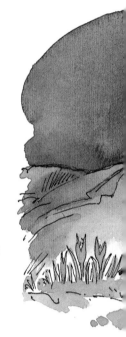

Der Frühling ist gekommen, und freudig
begrüßen ihn die Vögel mit heiterem Gesang.
Wenn die Zephirwinde schmeicheln,
murmeln süß die Quellen.

Wenn der Himmel sich in schwarz hüllt,
Blitz und Donner erschrecken,
verstummt der Vögel Gesang
und lebt im wiedergewonnenem Licht wieder auf.

Spring has come, and joyfully
The birds greet him with cheerful song.
As Zephyr's winds blow softly,
Brooks bubble sweetly.

When the heavens are veiled in darkness
And thunder and lightning break forth,
The birds cease their singing
Until the light returns once more.

I

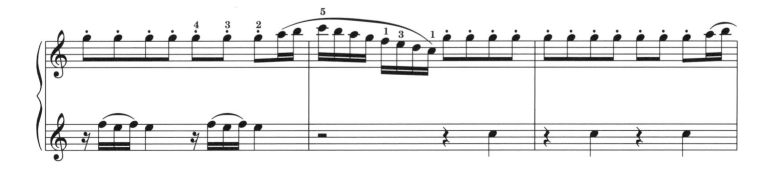

Und auf den lieblichen Blumenwiesen,
beim zarten Rauschen von Blättern und Pflanzen,
schlummert der Hirte, den treuen Hund zur Seite.

And on lovely meadows of flowers,
To the gentle rustling sound of leaves and plants,
The shepherd slumbers with his faithful dog at his side.

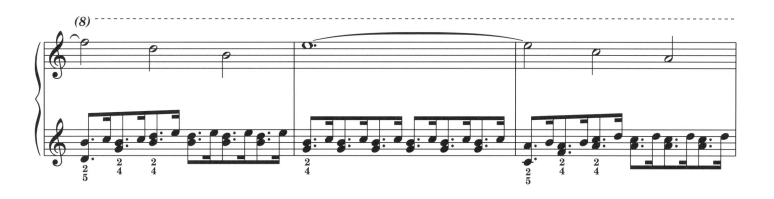

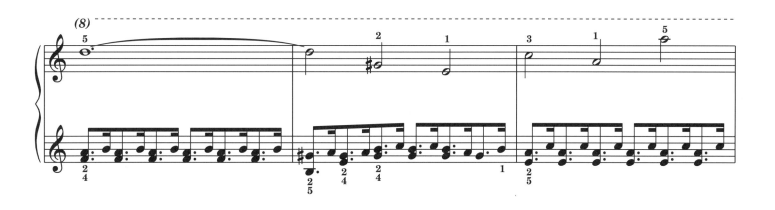

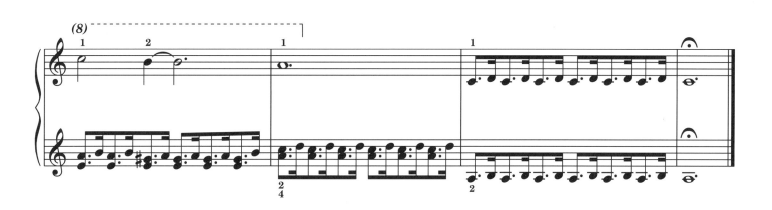

Zu ländlichen Dudelsackweisen
tanzen Nymphen und Hirten
unter dem leuchtenden Frühlingshimmel.

Nymphs and shepherds dance
To rustic bagpipe tunes
Under the bright spring sky.

III

Danza pastorale

Allegro ♩. = 66

L'estate
Der Sommer ‖ Summer)
op. 8/2

Unter der lastenden Hitze der Sonne
dürsten Mensch und Herde und versengt die Pinie:
Erhebt der Kuckuck die Stimme
und mit ihm singen Tauben und Stieglitz.
Der Zephirwind weht süß, aber auf einmal
bläst ihm der Nord ins Gesicht.
Es klagt der Schäfer, überrascht
vom wilden Sturm und seinem Geschick.

Under the burden of the sun's heat
Humans, flocks of sheep and pine trees are all parched:
When the cuckoo begins his song,
The doves and goldfinch join in chorus.
Zephyr's wind blows softly, but all at once
The North wind brings its icy blast.
The shepherd exclaims in dismay, surprised
By the misfortune of the sudden storm.

Allegro non molto ♩ = 66

Allegro ♩ = 116

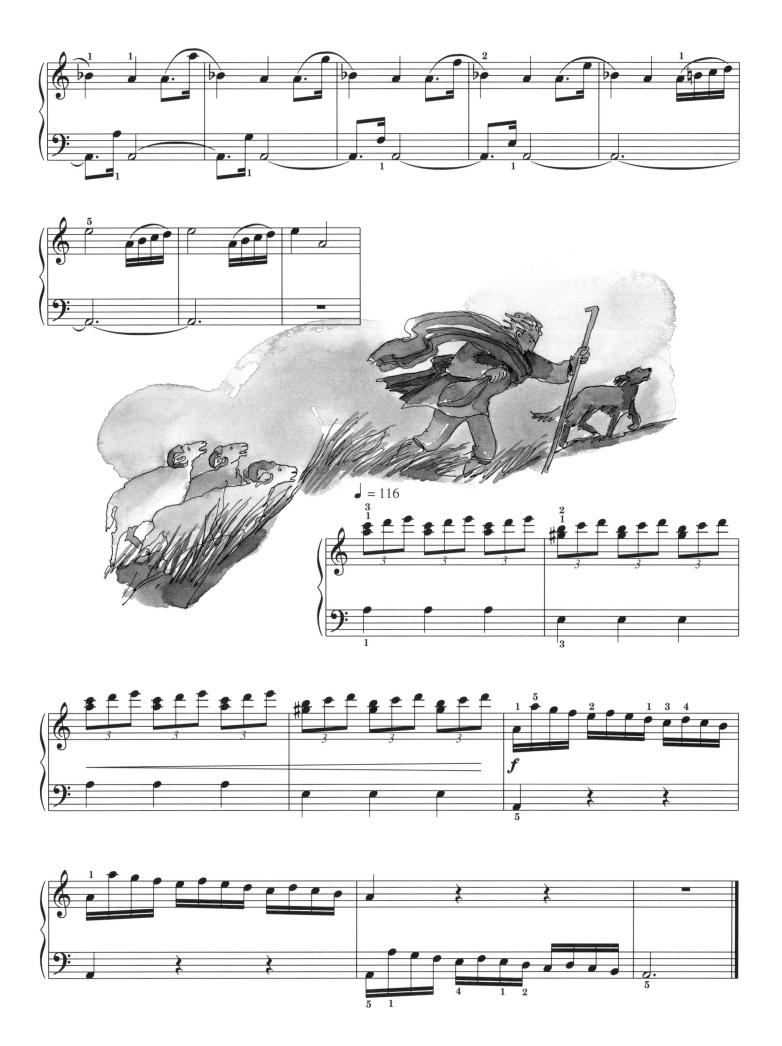

Von den Gliedern flieht der Schlaf,
aus Furcht vor Blitz und Donner,
vor Fliegen und Brummern.

All drowsiness is banished
By the fear of thunder and lightning,
At the approach of flies and bluebottles.

II

III

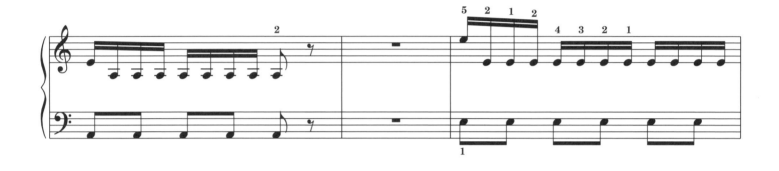

Ach, seine Furcht ist nur allzu wahr,
Donner und Blitze und Hagelschauer
vernichten Lavendel und Getreide.

Alas, he sees his fears come true,
As thunder, lightning and hailstones
Lay waste to lavender and corn.

L'autunno

Der Herbst ‖ Autumn
op. 8/3

Glücklich feiert der Bauer
mit Tanz und Gesang die gute Ernte,
und vom süßen Weine des Bacchus entflammt,
endet der Genuss im Schlummer.

Merrily the farmer celebrates
A good harvest with singing and dancing;
And soothed by the sweet wine of Bacchus,
The festivities end in slumber.

I

Larghetto ♪ = 80

II

Adagio molto ♩ = 50

So beschließen Tanz und Gesang
das Vergnügen.
Und die beginnende friedliche Zeit
lädt ein zu süßem Ruhen.

So the day's pleasures end
With singing and dancing,
And sweet repose invites
To a time of calm and quiet.

Das Tagesgrauen sieht den Aufbruch der Jäger,
mit Hörnern und Flinten eilen sie hinaus,
es flieht das Wild, sie verfolgen die Spur.
Schon erschreckt und ermattet vom Lärm
der Flinten und Hörner, verwundet
versucht es zu fliehen, muss jedoch sterben.

Dusk sees the huntsmen set out on their way,
Hurrying out with their horns and shotguns
On the track of their game as it flees.
Now frightened and exhausted by the noise
Of the shotguns and horns, the wounded animal
Tries in vain to escape, but has to meet its death.

III

La caccia

L'inverno
Der Winter ‖ Winter
op. 8/4

Zu gefrorenem Schnee erstarrend,
bei Kälte und grausamem Wind,
hackenschlagend, wärmesuchend,
zähneklappernd.

As snow freezes to ice
In the cold and bitter wind
We stamp our heels as we search for warmth,
With teeth a-chattering.

I

Allegro non molto ♪ = 120-132

II

Die Nähe des Herdes lockt.
Regenschauer vor den Fenstern.

The warmth of the stove is inviting.
Rain drums down outside the windows.

Das Eis verführt, doch die Furcht
einzubrechen, hält zurück.
Man stolpert, man fällt,
krachendes, brechendes Eis
mahnt zur Vorsicht.

The ice looks alluring, but the fear
Of falling through it restrains the skaters.
As they stumble and fall,
The cracks and breaks in the ice
Warn them to be careful.

Schott Music, Mainz 49 455

Im Ofenrohr balgen sich die Winde,
Sirocco, Bora und die anderen:
Leiden und Wonnen des Winters.

The winds whistle around in the stovepipe:
Sirocco, Bora and the others,
The trials and delights of winter.

ISBN-13: 978-1-4234-0814-7

Distributed By
HAL LEONARD

9 781423 408147

08739886

Fred Bock
Music
Company

www.FredBock.com

8739886 GERMAN CAROL FANTASY Organ BGK1029 $9.95

8 84088 03923 3

8

6

4

3

dedicated with gratitude to my friend, Margaret Anderson

GERMAN CAROL FANTASY

Sw.   Strings Sw. to Ch. 8'
Ch.   Strings, Flutes 8'
Gt.   Flutes 8', 4', trem.
Ped. 16', 8', Sw. to Ped.

Arranged by DIANE BISH

The Organ Music of

GERMAN CAROL FANTASY

Fred Bock Music Company

EXCLUSIVELY DISTRIBUTED BY
HAL•LEONARD